Nicholas Harlow

Nicholas Haslam
Sheer Opulence

Special Photography by David Montgomery

CICO BOOKS

London

To Min Hogg, my most beloved friend of a lifetime

First published in 2002 by Cico Books Ltd
32 Great Sutton Street London EC1V 0NB

10 9 8 7 6 5 4 3 2 1

A CIP catalogue record for this book is available from the British
Library

ISBN 1 903116 55 4

Additional text by Alex Parsons
Edited by Alison Wormleighton
Special photography by David Montgomery
Styling by Cynthia Inions
Designed by Christine Wood
Printed and bound in Singapore

Contents

Introduction

I became an interior decorator almost unintentionally. Although practically everything I had worked at in early adulthood involved "design" in some way, it wasn't until I turned thirty that I could truthfully use the words "Interior Designer" as my job description.

During my childhood, I contracted polio. I had to lie flat on my back for three years and could move only my arms. Though for the life of me I can't think why, my parents had a large-scale model house made by Lavender Herbert, the daughter of their great friend, the author and musician A. P. Herbert. The house could be pulled across my bed, and I would paint it and rearrange the furniture, constantly coming up with new decorative schemes for various imaginary inhabitants. My father's younger brother, Oliver, invented a wonderful mechanical theater; you just pressed a button and entire operas were played out on a tiny stage.

Vanity Fair Launch Party: for Tina Brown.

VANITY FAIR LETTERMEN

Nicholas Haslam February '90

I suppose that it is to him I owe my love of dramatic and theatrical effects – scenes that appear for a moment and then fade into one's memory.

When I finally went to school, I immediately decorated my regulation Eton study with fake ocelot-skin curtains, cut-paper ostrich-plume pelmets, and a carpet of artificial grass – what you could call "barococo-surreal." But I also created less over-the–top things, like sets for the school plays, and won most of the art prizes. In fact, the only good reports any tutor ever gave me were for art. So now, years later, I'm really just painting on much larger-scale canvases – interiors.

On leaving Eton I went to an art school near Bath, in the west of England. There weren't any interior design schools then, even if I'd thought about doing such a thing. I stood it for about

The
Cabinet
Room
Garden
House
Henley
on
Thames

Nicholas Haslam
1996

three weeks. The curriculum consisted of making things in raffia and papier-mâché, and there was I, wanting to be Toulouse-Lautrec.

I came back to London, gratefully mixing with contemporaries like Min Hogg (who was later to create the seminal magazine *The World of Interiors*), Christopher Gibbs, Terence Donovan, David Bailey, and Jean Shrimpton, plus many other upcoming artists, writers, and actors. Having been ill for so long in childhood, and seeing mostly people of my parents' age, I felt perfectly at ease with an older generation. Thus when I met their contemporaries – people like Lady Diana Cooper, Cecil Beaton, Oliver Messel, Bunny Roger, and Chips Channon, or the slightly younger David Hicks and Tom Parr – they all molded me, opened my eyes, taught me the point of the past, and encouraged me toward the future. Through them I saw amazing places – the great houses of England, France, and Italy, and not only rooms open to the public but ones that were private and personal. There was La Fiorentina, Rory Cameron's villa at Cap Ferrat, with the first "overflow" swimming pool and ravishing painted eighteenth-century furniture used with simple white rugs and works by Picasso and Braque.

And there was Simon Fleet's "Gothic Box," a minute, magical, cluttered Kensington *cottage orné*, where I realized that "junk" can be as pleasing and easy to live with as grand furnishings.

So the aesthetic I absorbed was rooted in the past. And what a great aesthetic it was. I saw splendor at its most glamorous and opulent, while being in the company of people who were going beyond the accepted boundaries of decoration and taste. The more experienced I get, the more I feel that in the eighteenth century taste reached its zenith – the beauty of furniture, objects, and porcelain, the wit and lightheartedness, the extraordinary gestures of extravagance. I love the idea of parterres of porcelain flowers at Versailles being changed in the course of a dinner in case people got bored seeing the same thing for too long; or a Russian prince sprinkling his garden with diamonds because it looked dreary; or plantation owners from the American Deep South illuminating their avenues with cages of fireflies. All very romantic, and I'm a very romantic decorator, but I also love the freshness of designers like Jean-Michel Frank, the simplicity of whitewashed villages, the drama of tribal art.

Beautiful beginnings

My parents had an exquisite house in Buckinghamshire, England, where I was born. Great Hundridge Manor (below) was the perfect example of countrified William and Mary architecture. The beautifully proportioned rooms with their painted paneling were brought to vibrant life by my father's cousin, the writer and amateur decorator Geoffrey Scott, author of *The Architecture of Humanism*. The house was sympathetically added to by Sir Clough Williams-Ellis, and the gardens designed by Cecil Pinsent. This team were the tastemakers of the

1920s, having famously created I Tatti, Bernard Berenson's Florentine *palazzino*. Their work was my earliest environment, and I suppose I just naturally assimilated the Renaissance style – strong and overscaled – that Geoffrey Scott employed at Hundridge (below). There were enormous sofas covered in white linen velvet, and toughly carved oak tables, over one of which, in the entrance hall, Geoffrey had fanned a faded viridian Elizabethan cloak edged in tarnished gold lace. There was romance and drama in every room, but all was very restrained and pure. I grew up thinking of interiors as works of art to be lived in, not bland backgrounds to be taken for granted. I realized that the key to a beautiful room is not so much an inventory of furnishings but the feeling that the space you are in is thrilling and yet harmonious.

From London to New York, Arizona, and Los Angeles, and the initial commission

The first house I decorated for myself was a run-down workman's estate cottage near London's Waterloo station, now a fearfully trendy area. It was really quite original, with my love of romance and scale shoehorned into its tiny rooms. There was a red "lacquer" sitting room – car paint, I seem to remember – and a brown linen oval-tented dining room, and I collected odd bits of furniture which I have to this day. My friends admired it, but it never occurred to me to decorate professionally. Instead I went to work on *Vogue* magazine in

Nicholas Haslam 1996

New York, moving apartments from time to time. Some were photographed for magazines, as they were so wacky compared with the prevailing American taste at that time. By then, I'd got to know some great style icons: Diana Vreeland, my boss at *Vogue*; the Duchess of Windsor; Andy Warhol; the great decorator Billy Baldwin. They were very complimentary, and when I moved once again to a duplex on 61st Street, I put together a drawing room that many people said was among the most beautiful they had ever seen.

After several dizzying years in the heaven that was New York in the 1960s, I was ready for a change from city life, from the magazine world, from parties and theaters. With a friend I found a ranch in Arizona, where we bred Arabian horses and ran a few head of cattle. The frankly hideous one-story ranch house got the full Haslam treatment, memories of Geoffrey Scott's Renaissance style being my inspiration. Many friends from Europe came to stay, amused by this gloriously atypical cowboy life. As Los Angeles was only a day's drive away, I also had a little house in Bel Air, where, while sometimes working as a photographer on

Dominic Dunne's movies, I decorated parties for film stars like Natalie Wood and Robert Wagner. But my freewheeling existence was now about to change. Alexander Hesketh, who had loved the 61st Street apartment and the ranch, bought a house in London and asked me to decorate it. So in 1972, after a decade in the United States, I returned home to take up, though little did I know it at the time, the profession of interior design.

The ethos of decoration

When I look at a room or house I've been asked to do, I know pretty well immediately how it should *look*, but more so how it should *feel*. If working from a plan, I need to maximize space and height and volume – often to be achieved by sleight of hand – before thinking of color and style. Clients will usually give me some indication of what they want, and I'll gradually tease more information from them, but if I don't think their ideas are appropriate to their lifestyle or

The Main Salon at Bellville Sassoon London SW1

Nicholas Haslam '91

the house's character, I'll gently steer them toward a different approach. Luckily, my clients generally become very close friends, so by the second or third job for them, I know them intimately. I always feel it is my role to surprise them with something they haven't dreamed of, but equally to surprise myself. I don't do "recipe" decoration, and often things change dramatically at the last minute, but I do know what I'm aiming for; I know about proportion, what's beautiful and exciting and what's not, and they have to trust me. There are things you just can't explain. Nancy Lancaster – John Fowler's partner in the decorating firm Colefax and Fowler, from the 1940s – once painted one room dusky pink and the next room a dirty blue, saying it wasn't the color of the rooms that mattered, but the color of the air between the rooms. Try explaining that to a client!

My philosophy is to listen carefully and then do exactly as I want. There's a great story I read on this subject. The famous architect Sir Edwin Lutyens was asked to build a vast house for an

Edwardian magnate. When going over the site with the client, Lutyens remarked, "And here there's going to be a black marble staircase." The client countered, "But I don't want a black marble staircase." Lutyens said, "Oh, what a pity." The client went off around the world during the house's construction, and came back to find it complete with the staircase. "I said that I didn't want a black marble staircase," he wailed. Lutyens replied, "And I said, what a pity."

Haslam style

There are so many rooms, houses, buildings, gardens, ruins, follies, cities, countries, and people that influence me. I sometimes get a crush on a particular place. At the moment I'm going through a big Russian/Prussian phase: St. Petersburg meets Potsdam. Luckily I have a photographic memory, and a huge, ever-expanding library of old and new reference books that constantly suggest ways of giving houses an imaginative twist of scale and surprise. I'm totally unafraid to juggle classical proportions to suit twenty-first-century requirements. All my favorite buildings have something slightly weird and wonky about them. I'm happy working in the modern idiom too, though I often find ultra-minimalism humorless and bland, like a too-perfect face. About twenty years ago I did my apartment all in steel and glass and black leather. It looked wonderful until one left clothes lying around, or put down a shopping bag. I aim to create rooms that somehow absorb the necessities of everyday life.

My taste in architecture stops somewhere around Istanbul or Damascus, where Christian happily mingles with Islamic. I prefer the European fantasies of Chinese, Japanese, or Indian buildings and interiors to the real thing: chinoiserie rather than chinois, if you like. Portuguese baroque is a favorite style of mine, as is that of the southern United States. They are both wonderful for houses in the sun. And I thought the houses I saw in Hollywood were amazing – the kind of homes where a Matisse would slide away and there'd be a movie screen behind it.

On the whole, I don't like elaborate oriental rugs, although I know a lot of people are very attached to them and I wouldn't part a client from a treasured possession. I prefer splashy, faded carpets – the simpler early Aubusson designs, for example, have an elegance that I feel got lost as the patterns became more elaborate. I'll design carpets myself if I can't get what I want for an interior, and I also design and make a lot of furniture. Apart from the rococo style, I don't really like eighteenth- and nineteenth-century English furniture when it is taken too seriously, especially dining tables and chairs. Too often, an English dining room ends up looking like a boardroom – acres of dark wood and a forest of angles. Someone once said that if you take English furniture abroad, say to France, it looks ludicrous, but French things

The entrance to
The Ballroom, The Savoy Hotel

by
Nicholas Haslam

THE ENTRANCE HALL
BY NICHOLAS HASLAM 1996

look wonderful wherever you put them. Maybe it's because the French furniture has fluid curves while the English pieces are generally rigid and stiff. I tend to deal with English furniture by painting it or adding slipcovers.

Painting wood is not as irreverent as it seems, unless it's mahogany. Wood paneling, for example, was always made to be gilded or painted. Originally, the furniture in grand houses was silvered, but when it was discovered that silver tarnished quite badly, gold was used instead. Gilvering – gold and silver rubbed together – is my favorite finish, and while it is hardly a bargain-basement option, it does looks stunning.

The
Drawing Room, at
Dean House, Kilmerston,
Nicholas Haslam

I'm not at all afraid to pastiche things, or mock things up like a stage set. I like curtains made from lining materials or cheap linen because they hold their folds and don't droop. One of my signature solutions is to use thick brown corrugated paper under the chair rail. It has a subtle serrated texture, and once it's been layered with color and lacquered, it makes a wonderful foil for the decorative wall coverings used above.

So many people are obsessed with getting back to the original, re-creating earlier centuries rigidly because they are afraid to break the rules. For the slavish, it's red damask or green damask and never prune-colored damask. Or it's heritage colors and never plain white – or

The Saloon, Gunton Park, Norfolk

Nicholas Haslam

what appears to be plain white but in my rooms is, in fact, myriad shades of white and off-white blended and rubbed together. People are too conventional when it comes to restoring houses, but they shouldn't be. Pioneers from the past like William Kent, Lord Burlington, and William Beckford in England, and the Gabriel brothers and Marie Antoinette's architect, Richard Mique, in France, broke rules to make the most extraordinary interiors. I'm sure that if plastic had been around in Marie Antoinette's day, she would have commanded someone to experiment with it.

My favorite materials are bronze, brêche violette marble, string-colored linen, white canvas, and painted wood that looks a bit wrecked and lived in. I like humor and wit, and on the whole

I don't like ditzy details unless they're married up to something tough, in which case a bit of ditz is like a touch of wit.

Scale is extremely important. I often overscale or underscale elements in a room to make them more interesting, to look grander or larger, or to make people feel more comfortable. One very good rule is to make furniture overscale for women so they feel cosseted, and to underscale it for men so they feel big and powerful. It's a subtle touch, and probably not politically correct, but it works.

The starting point and the finishing touch

Often I'll buy a key piece for a room, or I'll use something belonging to the client as a starting point and build from there. When I've got my ideas lined up, and a real grasp of the feeling I want for that room, I'll make a preliminary watercolor sketch to show how the room is going to look. The point of the sketches is to give everyone involved an idea of the bigger picture so that my team knows what we're working toward and the client knows what to expect.

My way of working means designing and making a great deal to order. Bit by bit I have found the best curtain makers, the best upholsterers, and a pair of magical specialist painters whose artistry you can admire throughout this book. An example of the genius of these people is that when I started, the artist Anish Kapoor used to make my furniture – those pieces would be exhibited in an art gallery now.

Decoration to me is about making people look prettier and feel happier. In the past, that was unashamedly the purpose of decoration. Consider a medieval hall as we see it today, with cold stone walls, bare flagstones, and light struggling through tiny windows. Now imagine it back in the Middle Ages, with colorful hangings, crackling fires, blazing candles, the sound of lutes, rugs underfoot, and every available surface, every coffered beam, patterned and gilded to reflect the light and enhance the complexion.

The eighteenth-century interior was also designed to flatter and please. The reflective surfaces – the mirrors, the silver, the gilding and painting – were there to enhance fire and candlelight, and they flattered the features in the same way as white ruffles at the throat and diamonds around the neck flatter the face.

I leave you with an image from the eighteenth century: a huge shallow glass bowl filled with water and exotic fish. The bowl is suspended from the ceiling by chains, candles flicker around the rim, and the gilded and painted ceiling dances with reflections from the rippling water for the delight of the assembled company. That's Sheer Opulence.

SPACE
Haslam style

My London apartment consists of four small rooms, which I originally painted white throughout and furnished with neutral colors to give a feeling of light and space. Recently, I had a change of heart and decided I wanted the apartment to work as a nighttime space. I used prune-colored paint on the walls with a sheen like the bloom on a grape, and covered the ceiling with a "mica" paper, lacquered to give it a moonlight glow. I love the result: the room looks like a nightclub in nineteenth-century Russia, had there ever been such a place.

The etching in a gold frame is a Graham Sutherland, and the classical torso and bust are plaster copies of the work of some long-forgotten master of the art of carving in marble. Classical statuary is an example of tough — as opposed to whimsical — detailing.

The curtains in the drawing room are made from inexpensive mauve cotton, and although they are pulling curtains, I rarely use them, preferring to regulate the light with slatted cedar blinds, which give a warm honey color to the air in the room. Inevitably, my own apartment is a place to experiment with ideas and also to use discards and leftovers from other jobs. The striped fabric on the table under the window is a case in point. A hand-painted trial for a fabric design, it's in exactly the right shades of brown and blue and has stripes that are just the right width to echo the slats of the blinds above. The other treat is a trio of beaded pillow covers made from the leftovers of the most wonderful tablecloth, which you can see on pages 146–147. The overall effect of the room is a cocooning space that is dark but rich, thanks to the palette of mauves and blues, with flashes of brilliant color and pools of light. The carpet is a neutral-colored wool, woven to look like sisal. When the room was painted white, the carpet looked creamy brown, but it now appears almost lilac.

This is a situation where one stunning image on the wall is enough. The image propped up under the table lamp is a parrot by Liz Butterworth.

The asymmetrical picture on the drawing room wall of my apartment was inspired by something I saw in the home of an art-collector friend. It was a tiny, jewel-like object by Jean Cocteau, his "signature" profile framing a minute Dali sketch of ruins. I had the frame made on a much larger scale and filled the space with photocopies of a Pannini etching and several coats of lacquer. I couldn't have a conventional light fixture dangling above such a romantic profile, so I made a surrealist chandelier out of a rusty anchor, a bunch of pear twigs, and some white spray paint. The cornice lighting is stunning in effect, but it could not be simpler. It's just a string of Christmas tree lights hidden behind the molding.

The sofas at this end of my drawing room are upholstered in linen, and the low table has a modern top supported by sea horses. One original sea horse was an eighteenth-century carving, but the cast copies are so good I've forgotten which leg is the real thing. The four upholstered stools, when grouped together, make a fake "Picasso." The sections were painted directly onto tough artists' canvas.

The table under the window at this end of the drawing room is a repository for beautiful objects and personal icons. In the center is the British pop star Liam Gallagher, and on the far right, under the Giacometti-style table lamp, is Elsie de Wolfe, the influential American decorator of the 1930s and friend of the Duchess of Windsor.

At the far end of my drawing room, the furniture is darker and the atmosphere warmer. The gothic chairs, which I love, are upholstered in Louis Vuitton fabric, as used for their suitcases. The low table is black lacquer and the sofa is covered in purple-brown velvet and fur, its shade of brown chosen to complement all the shades of mauve, plum, and lilac. The paintwork on the Dutch cupboard and on the pretty French chair has been deliberately left scruffy.

The wallpaper in the study was originally painted by George Oakes, who worked with John Fowler, and it is all the decoration a wall needs. The low table has been converted from an eighteenth-century dog bed, and the rug is an ordinary white flokati.

TOWN
glamour

My previous London apartment was a very glamorous place. I played up the strengths of the original period detailing and made the space a celebration of European decoration at its most outlandish, with a different source of inspiration for each room. The octagonal entrance hall/dining room was made to look as if the rococo Amalienburg pavilion had become a ruin (see pages 106–107), while the drawing room was inspired by a nineteenth-century Russian watercolor. My bedroom was a version of my father's bedroom in our seventeenth-century home in Buckinghamshire, England. The bathroom had a French theatrical feel, and the kitchen was reminiscent of a nineteenth-century Normandy dairy. The room I liked best was my study, with its lovely faded toile de Jouy fabrics, hand-painted chinoiserie wallpaper, and pretty French furniture.

The two rooms that form the main drawing room area are treated as one, with the same black curtains and faux finish to the walls, which are painted to resemble milk glass. The eighteenth-century chairs — painted, of course — are a mix of the real and the faithful copy.

The drawing room of the apartment was inspired by rooms at the palace of Pavlovsk, outside St. Petersburg. Named after its first owner, the eighteenth-century Russian emperor Paul, the palace in its turn was inspired by an Imperial Grand Tour of Europe in the 1780s, when it was built. What makes the palace of Pavlovsk so interesting is that it's a view of eighteenth-century European style through Russian eyes – and the palace is filled with exquisite, strong detailing the royal travelers re-created when they came home, using the superb heritage of Russian craftsmanship on European design.

My drawing room is dominated by a Venetian portrait that hung in my father's house. Underneath sits an eighteenth-century French daybed upholstered in mauve damask and flanked by modern brass-rail tables topped with a pair of delicate urn lamp bases. There is another huge urn in the doorway, standing grandly on a column that is an eighteenth-century original. The doorway on the right affords a glimpse of the curtains: dramatic floor-to-ceiling black linen, with a trim of toile de Jouy. The stiff pelmet is inset with Leonardo engravings. It is amusing to think that an identically shaped apartment in the same block was owned by the architect John Pawson, king of minimalism.

My father's bedroom in our house in Buckinghamshire had the most extraordinary "grotesque" paneling. Echoing it, I used a paint effect that looks like antique marble, with a panel over the bed dissolving into a monochrome landscape. Deviating from the original a bit here, I've put in a reference to my own place in the country, an early eighteenth-century hunting lodge with a "Jacobean" façade (see pages 34–37). The bed, which is Italian, is painted a dull olive green. The bedspread is a rust-colored rep that warms the walls, as do the red lampshades.

The bathroom is totally theatrical. The freestanding marbleized bath is framed by a pair of tattered, hand-painted John Fowler curtains that I found abandoned in a shed at the hunting lodge. The table came from a yacht and the wall behind the table has been marbleized to pick up the colors of the bath and the Fortuny fabric on the footstools. The suitably dramatic centerpiece is a terra-cotta Virgin and Child with swirling drapery. The lamp bases are severely classical black granite urns topped with drum shades in toile de Jouy.

The bedroom curtains, above left, are made from white
canvas looped onto a rod that runs the length of the window
wall. The fabric between the windows is an original Colefax
and Fowler design. The oriental rug is nicely faded and the
curvaceous gilt chairs are Italian.

In the bathroom, pictured above, the one object that almost distracts the
eye from the Virgin Mary is the silver ewer placed by the faucets.
It was a very ugly brass object from Morocco, but once silvered it
became beautiful.

The sofa in the sitting room of my country home is upholstered in an early John Stefanidis fabric, and the low table is a Victorian stool with painted legs and a top of needlepoint stitched by me. The black blob is my Pekinese, Zandonai, named after a follower of Puccini. All my dogs have had names beginning with "Z" and I am beginning to scrape the bottom of the barrel.

OPULENCE
in the country

The place I escape to at weekends is a hunting lodge that originally belonged to John Fowler, the genius who, with Sybil Colefax, in the 1930s founded the decorating firm of Colefax and Fowler, which epitomized the English Country House look. The sitting room is tiny but perfect. I do not generally like to put pictures or mirrors over a mantelpiece, as it is too predictable, but I broke my own rule with the picture of St. Thomas of Copertino levitating. Fittingly, as there is an RAF helicopter base nearby, he is the patron saint of pilots.

The collection of sepia engravings on the wall behind the console table in the sitting room is part of a job lot acquired for five pounds (about seven dollars). Properly mounted and framed grandly in gilt, they look magnificent.

The paint on the walls in the sitting room is the traditional Suffolk pink that was used on outside walls to keep the flies more interested in staying outside than buzzing around in the house. It worked because the paint mixture, which was reapplied regularly, was made up of distemper and fresh bull's blood. This paint, which has been on the walls for years, has lost its attraction for blood-sucking insects, and has faded elegantly to a washed-out, faded brown-rose.

The lodge needed a small touch of full-on grandeur, so a rather good terra-cotta bust of Marie Antoinette graces the console table. She is the perfect color for the walls and the soft gilded wood of the old frames behind her.

The staircase in this entrance hall is a mélange of stylistic ideas, in this case a blend of French and English classicism. The design of the balustrade is drawn from an eighteenth-century "fer forgé" (wrought iron) pattern book, so the stairs give a French sweep to a classic English entrance hall. Architectural elements such as door frames and cornices are deliberately overscaled to make the entrance doubly imposing.

THE HOUSES
and their rooms

The entrance hall of this town house is all brand-new but has the patina of aged grandeur. It is pretty and welcoming without being fussy.

RUSSIAN fantasy

A London town house is a wonderful brief for a decorator. You have restrictions of space and light that you don't get in the country, and restrictions tend to make one more inventive. It is also a great opportunity to do something lavish and grand. There's one London town house I've decorated for three different clients, so I've become very familiar with its moods and metamorphoses. On the last occasion, I was asked to add to the decorations in the entrance hall and to turn the basement bedroom into a dining room. I had just returned from a visit to Russia and my head was full of the harmonious beauty of Pavlovsk, which is, in fact, quite a small palace as palaces go, but gives the impression of a majestic and monumental construction.

The entry hall is marbled and gilded, and even though everything in it is new, it looks as if it had been around since the days of Imperial Russia. The radiator has been boxed in with an old altar rail that has been gilded and rubbed back to look dull and worn, with a top made from a chipped piece of rough-hewn, unpolished marble. The gilt-framed *verre églomisé* (gilded glass) mirror, which I had made, is tipped forward to reflect the staircase.

*T*he chandelier hangs over the serving table, the chain covered with a red grosgrain sleeve, and a generous rosette hides its anchorage to the ceiling. The rest of the overhead lighting is provided by four identical silver lanterns, the corner of one of which you can just see at the top left of the photograph (see also page 165).

I altered the apparent proportions of the dining room by putting in overscaled columns and

pillars. They are made from wood and plaster painted to look like the finest rose-colored

marble. The panels on the doors are also overscaled – the bronze roundel below the handle is

the size of a dinner plate. I covered the Chippendale chairs with slipcovers of figured white

cotton because I didn't want any dark, hard geometry in this romantic room. The sparkle

comes from the bead-embroidered tablecloth. In the mirror, you can see a chinoiserie panel

inspired by the little Chinese Palace at Oranienbaum, near St. Petersburg. The panel is made

of silver mica paper painted to look like beadwork.

The dining room in this gracefully proportioned London apartment has a silver shimmer and accents of pink and green. None of the patterns "match" or "coordinate"; they just look as if they were made to be together.

GRACIOUS
living

The apartment pictured here and on the following pages is perhaps one of the best-shaped apartments in London – the proportions and spaces are wonderful to work with and it was a real pleasure to decorate. For the dining room, I took as my starting point the amusing chinoiserie panels the clients had brought from their home in California. Having found a scrap of eighteenth-century hand-painted paper that I really liked, I wanted to produce the effect without slavishly re-creating the paper, so I had a cheap textured wallpaper silvered and the design painted over the silvering. Thus we were able to place the elements of the pattern exactly where we wanted them. I commissioned the plaster overdoors to work with the swirling design while putting the chinoiserie firmly in an eighteenth-century London town house context.

The mirrors over the sideboard were handmade to an eighteenth-century design, with tiny gilt studs at the junctions of the panels and a painted wood frame matching the painted sideboard. This is a perfect surface to display the owners' collection of very good silver. All other objects are white, which is one of my passions.

The dining room has a wonderful romantic feel to it. It's full-on glamorous, filled with beautiful silver, and the air practically shimmers. Although the room has excellent proportions, I felt that they could be improved and so I created a fake door for balance. In the photograph, it's the one on the left. The doors are painted with countless shades of off-white to suggest a patina normally achieved by a hundred years of good cigar smoke. Between the chair rail and the baseboard I used MDF (medium-density fiberboard), painted to look like paneling, with silvery-green "wood planks" and silver "nail heads." The table was made for the room out of old oak, which has more depth than mahogany. The chairs were originally upholstered in a darker, striped velvet. The chintz slipcovers were the clients' brilliant idea – a change that pulled the whole room together.

The chandelier was the clients' own. I painted some of the droplets with mauve and amber paint and had the tassel specially made from silver rope. Crystal beads

An enfilade — a succession of rooms that open into one another through wide double doors — as left, is a perfect arrangement for entertaining, as it turns the entire apartment into one circulation space.

Overleaf: The drawing room in the same apartment. Painting a grand and glamorous room white is not as simple as it looks. This effect is built up with fourteen different shades of white.

Rooms should each have their own character, but they still have to work together. This view of the enfilade from the entry hall, through the leather-walled library to the silver and chinoiserie dining room, shows how it can be achieved. Each room has the same feeling of muted grandeur, slightly *délabré*. All the ceilings have elaborate cornicing. In the dining room, I painted the cornicing white to concentrate attention on the hand-painted wallpaper. In the library, I had the cornice decoration picked out in gilt and then lacquered until it looked suitably aged. The effect was to carry the gleam of the stamped and gilded leather on the walls right up to the ceiling.

I like to mix furniture styles. If they're interesting pieces, they'll go together. For example, in the photograph on the left, there's a 1920s Japanese black lacquer desk, a French bergère chair, and, on the back wall of the dining room, part of a suite of late eighteenth-century Venetian commodes with the original faux wood-graining.

The entrance hall, shown left, is based on an idea from the Russian palace of Pavlovsk. All the elements are overscaled. The urn illuminates the mirror surface, which slopes backward, drawing the eye upward. Even the doorknob is large — about 9 inches (23cm) across. The result is a small entrance hall that looks and feels monumental.

The fire basket in the library, right, is unique iron rococo, and in front stands a Chinese lacquer box. The marble fireplace surround is an early Italian bolection molding, with no shelf to attract anything that might disrupt the elegant sweep upward.

The white drawing room has touches of gilding, white ornaments, and curtains of heavy white silk over thin white taffeta, over unlined mauve taffeta. The checked, striped, and patterned upholstery fabrics are in muted shades of gray and lilac. Traditional yet unexpected touches are a leopardskin velvet stool and a huge terra-cotta urn.

For the library, I chose a stamped and gilded leather wall covering and put a pair of similarly colored nineteenth-century French salon chairs in front of the fireplace. Going for grandeur, I had bookcases made for the four corners of the room, with overscaled overdoors and blank roundels above, the proportions of which matched those of the plaster plaque above the mantel. The bookcase to the left of the fire is, in fact, a door to another part of the apartment. I've used dull, rich colors. The eighteenth-century stool is covered in very distressed red velvet and the sofa in a mole-colored cane-weave silk. The carpet is an early Aubusson, as is the tapestry pillow. Early Aubusson I love, but I find the later designs too flimsy.

The library pictured above is in a house in the country. The design is based on the massive Great Hall at Castle Howard in England but is contained along two sides of a corridor less than 8 feet (2.5 meters) wide. The area beyond the bookcases is the place to read and relax.

Adapting proportions is what my decorating is about. The photographs center and right are of the drawing room of a London town house. Untypically, the room is long and narrow, with a large bay window facing the garden. In order to make the room feel more balanced, I changed the focal point from the window to the center of the room by putting a large white plaster overmantel above the stone fireplace, to reflect light and attract the eye. In the placement of furniture, I again focused attention around the center of the room, achieving comfort without blocking the flow of circulation.

In the library, far left, the eye is drawn onward and upward by the overscale columns with their gilded flutes leading to the arched window at the far end. The large stone urn is the perfect termination of the view.

The plaster overmantel above the fireplace in the center and right-hand pictures is the main device used to change one's perception of the proportions; I try to avoid the cliché of mirrors and pictures over fireplaces. The walls in this room are covered in velvet with applied velvet panels outlined by wool-like silk fringing. The hard pelmets are of striped silk with a mauve and gilt metal fringe, but the curtains are made from an inexpensive beige linen which folds dramatically. The shades of brown and taupe chosen for the room are relaxing, easy to live with, and particularly flattering in lamplight.

The huge standing mirror, left, that sits on the draped table in the entrance hall is very grand. It was probably from a church altar.

In the entrance hall, right, the ornaments are white, the orchids are artificial, and the elegant lantern is black metal.

Overleaf: The orange theme in the drawing room was picked up from the owner's painting by the Italian painter Canale.

CLASSIC
and contemporary

As you walk through the front door of this London mansion apartment, you step into a warm *palazzo*. The entrance hall is divided by a pair of sweeping white silk noile curtains, held back low down with large tassels. I draped the undistinguished staircase that leads up to the mezzanine floor with white fabric, an idea I got from Christian Dior's own house in Paris. The wood banisters have been painted to look like bronze, and now the stairs have dramatic flair. The table in the entrance hall (right) faces the dining room and is covered in a padded cloth so there is little wood. The *palazzo* feeling is reinforced by faux marble paintwork and a classical bust. Because the drawing room is enormous, I added columns and trees to create a diversion in the middle (see overleaf). The hexagonal table in the center, like the table in the entrance hall, has an elaborately fringed cloth of cream silk.

The whiskey-colored walls in the drawing room look great at night, when pools of light are created by the lamps and wall lights.

The walls of this room are painted with a color that looks like a glass of whiskey held up to the light, and the curtains are a transparent whiskey color, lit low from behind so they glow at night as well as when the sun shines through them.

At the other end of the room is a cabinet, fronted with chicken wire, with a painted pediment. I found the original pediment in a garden shed. The cabinet has been painted with several shades of white and off-white. All the sofas in the room are very large – in this scale of room a small sofa would look lost. Dark woods would not suit this idiom, so most of the furniture is either cloth-covered or painted.

It could almost be the salon of a French château, but this is an entrepreneur's retreat in a London pavilion.

A relaxed, comfortable feel with a touch of wit was required for this little pavilion set in a private garden in central London. There was no need for curtains to provide privacy, and it was not an environment that called for swathes of fabric – it needed to be more simple and masculine than that. I used a fabric called Eclipse, which is a dirty gold/dirty silver metallic material made for photographers' lighting. It hangs beautifully because although the fabric is thin, it has a fluidity to it. The curtains hang from large-scale gilded rods that take the eye upward. I used faux stone for the walls, in bands like on the exterior of Parisian houses.

Flanking the French Provençal mirror is a pair of simple French 1940s gilt-bronze appliques (see page 166) with candles. The table lamp base is one of a pair of draped black urns that echo those on the gilded appliques. The tables at either side of the marble fireplace are made deliberately overscale, while the bronze-and-glass low table is uncompromisingly modern. The chairs by the fireplace are covered in beige silk, with pillows of pink striped French silk, and the two slipper chairs are upholstered with a cut velvet. The beiges, rusty browns, and creams of the upholstery look luxurious against the robust faux stonework.

*oft lighting and fresh flowers
create an irresistible ambience.
Real candles flicker in the French
1940s gilt-bronze appliques, and a beaten-pewter
vase throws back the gleam of firelight.*

Interiors can be so inviting, with soft, flattering colors like beiges and pinks, lights that gleam

rather than glare, and furniture that invites relaxation. The clichéd high-comfort interior is

one with remote-controlled dimmer lights and wall-to-wall black leather, but I can't see its

appeal. Far more attractive is the caress of silk and fur or the flicker of candlelight on a warmly

colored wall. The interior of this little city pavilion is a good example. People look and feel good

in this space because the colors are relaxed and the scale of the architectural elements

defines the room.

The dining room in the pavilion is dominated by a painting of a Neapolitan fisherman. His silvery catch and the hints of deep pink fit the color scheme perfectly.

The stairs lead directly from the drawing room. I created a pair of solid gilded columns to disguise the banal banisters of the staircase and to lead the way to the bedroom via a zebra stair carpet.

This amusing bust, left, stands on a pedestal in the entrance hall. It looks like stone layered with lichen but is, in fact, made of papier-mâché and was probably used as a stage prop.

A view of the entrance hall, right, looking through to the drawing room. It had a dull modern tile floor, which I changed to wide, waxed antique oak boards more sympathetic to the gentle country garden surrounding the house. The curtains are a simple glazed Nicholas Haslam linen, edge-to-edge lined in water-green.

COUNTRY
idyll

I was recently asked to do a mill house in Hampshire which had once been decorated by the legendary John Fowler, the interior decorator most renowned for redefining the English Country House look – that harmonious simple elegance that is so marvelously easy to live with and pleasing to the eye. Every sign of John Fowler's influence had long since disappeared, but I thought this project a perfect opportunity to pay homage to Fowler's style.

The mill house is documented in the Domesday Book, and though it retains several of the original small rooms with low, beamed ceilings, larger rooms have been added over the centuries. A river meanders around the outside of the house, effectively creating an island, and the millstream rushes under the entry hall, which is where the mill wheel once stood. One of my main aims was to bring in light, with subtle echoes of the shimmering water outside.

There are no garish notes in this drawing room. The colors all look as if they had been assembled for decades. Above right, you can see the subtle shades of silk used for the pillows: khaki, dull yellow, and a dusty orange-pink. The double doors, above left, lead from the entry hall into the drawing room. The finger plates, handles and lock cases, which are mainly Queen Anne, Georgian, and Victorian, are deliberately not uniform.

The drawing room has that soft look of having evolved over time and is reminiscent of John Fowler's work in the 1960s. The walls are painted in mauve-brown *faux bois* (wood-graining), with the grain of the wood picked out in silver, which catches the ripples of the stream outside the French doors. The curtains are of mauve cotton with a secondary set of filmy, pale pinkish-mauve unlined silk. The pair of English bergères are upholstered in a heavy strié cotton taffeta, and the chintz-covered sofas are outlined with a thick caterpillar fringe to give them definition. The flattering mauve/silver palette is balanced by a pewter-colored linen velvet carpet. An early Aubusson rug and a Victorian beaded needlework stool add splashes of warm color and the essential touches of black. Amateur hand-drawn marine maps of Europe and North America in tough, dull-gilded baroque frames, and colored engravings of strange shell prints that look surprisingly modern, add to the aqueous theme.

In the dining room, the furniture is painted white and set against walls of very pale gray-green faux paneling. For fun, I placed the Georgian overdoor on top of the dark, brooding Elizabethan oak cupboard, which the owners already possessed. It added height as well as humor and so has remained there.

This dining room is arranged for the display of an 80-piece set of 1760 Ludwigsburg porcelain that I found in Paris. As the dishes were handmade, they are all slightly irregular in shape and size, and each one is decorated with a different claret-colored bouquet of tulips and roses. It is the most beautiful porcelain I have ever seen and I decorated the room around it. The classical dark-green and gilded side tables were bought from Christie's of London. The owners had the pair of delightfully beaten-up stools with leather seats to put under them (one seen here), which prevented the tables from looking too formal.

In the bedroom, left, the carpet, which is the same as that used in the entry hall and on the stairs, looks like moss. The bed area is defined with a luxurious white silk rug. Italian wall lights in a bathroom, above, flank an antique Swedish mirror. I designed the marble surround of the sink, setting it above a noile skirt.

In the principal bedroom, a pretty nineteenth-century French carved bed is painted a dull green. Chintz is used for the footboard but on the corona it is interspersed with ribbons of prune-colored watered silk. These echo the strips of Mauny border on the duck-egg blue walls. The fabric lining the corona and covering the headboard is a pale prune/green shot taffeta. The walls of the bathroom are covered in a lilac-and-green Mauny paper.

*This romantic little bedroom
has a wonderful Elizabethan
four-post bed, which I lined
and tented in sheer white voile, and
walls washed a pale gray-violet.*

In this New Orleans French Quarter house, the entrance hall is dominated by the staircase. The delicate chandelier is a perfect find. Of unknown origin, it came from an antique shop in New York.

SOUTHERN
comforts

This homage to myriad European architectural styles lies behind a pink stucco balconied façade in the French Quarter of New Orleans. The eighteenth century was the main source of inspiration, but with an added touch of élan, glamour, and drama. The understated entrance hall has a staircase of white stone with a "traditional" iron railing forged to my design and finished in a very dark blue with a faux bronzed handrail. The scarlet curtains are made from British guardsmen's cloak material trimmed with brown grosgrain.

The small book-lined dining room, pictured overleaf, with its narrow columns, storm-cloud ceiling, and icon is based on the Tsar's Bedroom in the Catherine Palace near St. Petersburg. The faux tortoiseshell dining chairs have trellis backs and are upholstered in a cerulean blue trellis pattern to bring the painted sky color down to earth.

The salon, shown on pages 83–85, is dominated by spectacular chinoiserie wallpaper hand-painted by Paul and Janet Czainski, who flew out from London to do this. We first put up a gold paper, then oiled it to give it a dull sheen, and the design, inspired by a castle outside Potsdam, Germany, was painted on top.

Mirror panels in the corners give the book-lined dining room, left, interesting perspectives, and at night they augment the play of candlelight.

The matching chandeliers, seen from the salon, right, have a very Russian Imperial look to them. Using two together in a small space is an extravagant gesture that works. The armchairs, which are covered in a shiny metallic silk, pick up the sheen of the wallpaper.

Overleaf: The glorious salon.

The salon is breathtaking. The decoration is a fusion of European eighteenth-century interiors. The design of magnolias on the wallpaper, taken from a hunting schloss, is also echoed in the upholstery of the pair of painted armchairs. The sofa is covered in a thick white duchesse satin and the fireside chairs in a dusty mauve velvet. Below the chair rail, I have used thick brown corrugated paper that has been lacquered. The huge chandelier is Italian, holds sixty candles, and can be winched down from the ceiling. Again this is a room with no wood showing except for the floor; every chair and table has been painted or gilded or both. The console table on the far wall serves as a bar and was made to order. Its distressed paintwork is repeated on the chairs.

The walls and ceiling of this London drawing room are painted the color of linen, with the cornice picked out in a darker shade to draw the eye upward. The effect is grand but very restrained and coolly glamorous.

Overleaf: A fusion of violet and cream in the drawing room echoes the peace of the park it overlooks.

ESTABLISHED and eclectic

Diana Vreeland, the doyenne of American fashion, lived in this house overlooking London's Regent's Park during the 1930s. In her day it was decorated largely in her favorite red lacquer. It has high ceilings, and the drawing room has floor-to-cornice French doors that open onto a balcony.

I wanted a glamorous treatment for this house – glamorous with an edge and not a hint of chintz. The drawing room is an imposing "L" shape. In consultation with the client, we decided on a palette of white, beige, brown, and gold, underpinned by my favorite mauve and a touch of pink. Every room should have something pink in it, because it makes all the other colors sing.

The drawing room, an "L" shape, has two fireplaces; this one, left, is in the smaller part of the "L." The dark urns repeat the decorative iron fireback. The cabinet to the left of the fire is English, painted with a shabby black lacquer. The French chairs are gilded and very lightly distressed.

The furniture in the drawing room is deliberately simple because I did not want to detract

from the curtains, which are the pièces de résistance. I am not normally in favor of swags,

but in this case I wanted to add interest to the top part of the high-ceilinged room and that

meant putting strong detail in the pelmets. I chose a thick silk to hang in straight folds – no

tie-backs – with undercurtains in a dirty mauve shade. I turned the cascades around

so the linings show; the cascades are held onto the swagged pelmet by knots of fabric

known as choux.The carpet is linen, the upholstery fabric velvet, and the club fender is

covered in mauve suede. I added a twig table, a copy of a late 1930s French table, as a

touch of wit and a reminder of the trees in Regent's Park outside the windows. The portrait

by Van Dongen (see page 88) is, appropriately, beige and mauve.

A room like this requires restraint with flowers and objects. The touches of silver, the peach-colored roses, and the purple grape hyacinths are all that is needed.

The dining room of the Regent's Park house has a Colefax and Fowler painted paper on the walls. I wanted to make the room the color of a cloud, restricting the color range to grays and off-whites. The mirror over the fireplace was originally gilded, which looked too brash, so I painted it. I also painted the Chippendale-style dining chairs, which took some courage, but I think they look much better now and they work well in this room, which has grandeur with a modern edge.

The mirror-topped dining table was a favorite device of Elsie de Wolfe. This one was inspired by that of the Duke and Duchess of Windsor in Paris. At elegant dinners it adds to the sparkle of silver, crystal, candlelight, and beautiful people.

The right-hand side of this room is open to a covered terrace, and sea breezes blow through. The room is informal in intent and style, though disciplined in arrangement. The coral-colored sofa adds a touch of sophistication with its gilded tassels, but the painted bamboo furniture is covered with a simple cotton stripe.

SUNLIGHT
and shadow

In the 1950s the celebrated theatrical designer Oliver Messel transformed the storeroom of Leamington Great House in Barbados into a charming beach pavilion in the Portuguese baroque taste. Several years later, the pavilion was enlarged into a separate house. The present owners wanted to extend it farther while retaining elements of the original theatrical feel. I decided to keep the pavilion's strict architectural form, creating a European backdrop for the distinctly casual Bajan poolside life. The drawing room has walls of coral stone with a door in each corner. I added the overdoors and hung a pair of huge eighteenth-century Italian paintings as focal points.

The covered terrace outside the drawing room of the beach pavilion is a place to cool off from the sun. The space has a consciously Oliver Messel feel to it. I copied the trelliswork from a garden room at Badminton, England. I hung lanterns from mauve ribbons and covered the curved seating in sea-green cotton with pillows in cool water-ice shades.

The indoor-dining part of the drawing room, left, has simple, formal furniture under the painting, and glimpsed through the doorway is a faux eighteenth-century "set piece" with Chinese ginger jars.

Open to the breeze, the principal bedroom, right, has walls of coral stone and a marble floor. The four-post bed is a version of the eighteenth-century Italian style. The table is local in origin, and nineteenth century in design.

The principal bedroom was kept architecturally simple but the four-post bed is grandly proportioned. The play of scale is a favorite trick, but it works particularly well here.

The great dining room (pictured overleaf) has been described as the most beautiful room in Barbados. The coral stone walls are washed with paint the color of seawater, which gives off an iridescent glow at night. Figures representing the seasons stand in the corner recesses. I framed them with local shells, then sprayed coral dust over the shells so they don't look real at all but like elaborate carving. The table is hand carved and painted and has a mirror top, another glamorous touch picked up from the Windsors' home in Paris.

At night-time the dining room sparkles with light from the candles on the table, the delightfully wonky chandelier, and the wall lights, which have mirrored backs.

The chair frames match the table, but their short white skirts give them humor. At the far right of the room, the elaborate "Austrian stove" is painted white and dirty silver. A fake, it hides the stereo.

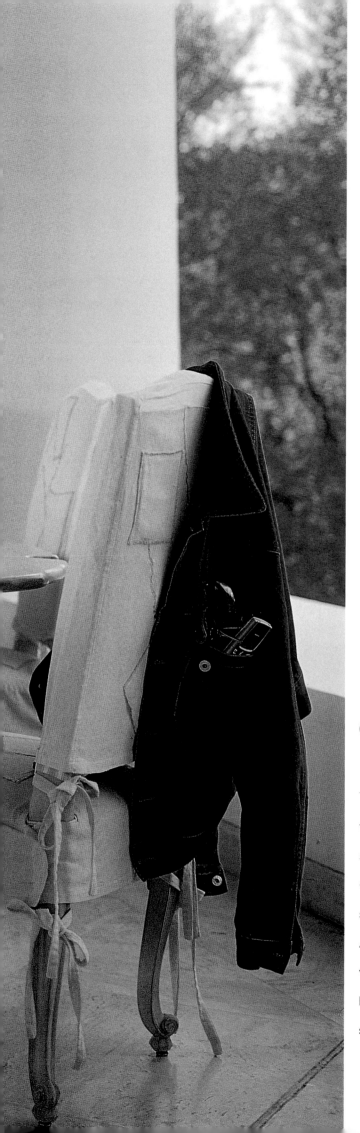

This "ruin" table is in a portico of a villa overlooking the sea on Cap Ferrat, France. The table comprises three pieces, which are fitted together to make one large surface. The chairs are elegant Louis XV but, in keeping with the theme of lost splendor, their slipcovers are artfully torn and patched.

MEDITERRANEAN
evening

The "ruin" table is an artful conceit. The broken giant capitals and tumbled columns are made of carved wood painted to look like stone. The jumble of architectural elements evokes a stylized, Classical but decadent elegance, and it was just the right kind of strong outdoor furniture that this colonnaded portico required. Anything in bamboo, wicker, or wrought iron would have looked too weak. The table divides into three, so it can be used either as one large surface or as a smaller one with serving consoles. The three sections are on runners so they are easy to move.

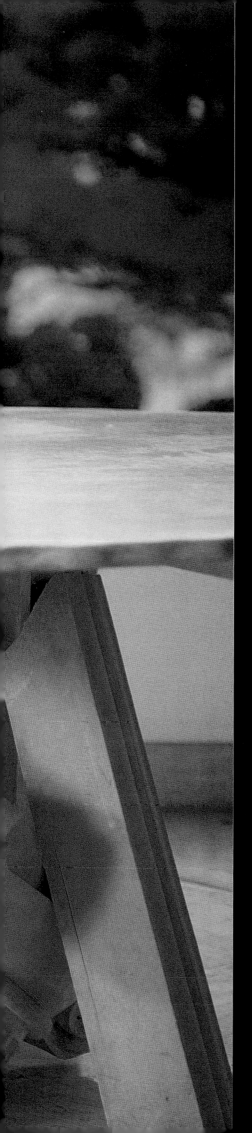

The "ruin" table, here in its smaller incarnation. The other two sections have been moved inside to the adjoining room. The portico feels cool, spare, and white, like a forum in the ancient world.

The panel above the doors to the right has faux charred remnants of a pretty floral painting as a reminder of the grandeur of earlier days. The gilt clock is poignantly stopped at 4:55 — the moment the Paris mob stormed Versailles during the French Revolution.

REVOLUTION
style

The rococo Amalienburg pavilion in the grounds of the Nymphenburg Palace, near Munich, was the inspiration behind the entrance hall/dining room in my previous London apartment. I wanted a room that worked best at night, and I decided that a ruined version of Chips Channon's famous Amalienburg dining room would be an amusing conceit. The room was, in fact, square, and in turning it into an octagon I hid windows behind some panels and serving cupboards behind others. The room has a wonderfully tragic, romantic feel. Storm clouds are gathering on the ceiling and what look like heavily distressed mirrored walls are sheets of oiled silver paper with silver-painted glazing bars over the top. The cornice evokes shattered glass with brickwork peeking through, and the final touch is a blast of realistic spray-on cobwebs.

A classically proportioned archway leads from the principal bedroom in a London apartment to dressing rooms and a private sitting room beyond, where the wallpaper is an American 1830s design that is amazingly cubist and modern.

SEDUCTION by decoration

Bedrooms should be relaxing, pretty rooms, neither too feminine nor too masculine. The colors should be flattering to the skin and the textures sensuous. The bedroom pictured here and overleaf fulfills all these criteria. This is the principal bedroom in a large apartment in London's Belgravia. The broken-pediment overdoor was copied from Claydon, a ravishing chinoiserie house in Buckinghamshire that I remembered visiting in my childhood.

The Nicholas Haslam wall covering is printed cotton in a design I adapted from a scrap of nineteenth-century fabric. I changed the original pinks and browns to blues and grays to give it a washed-out Swedish feel and used a linen-colored paint on the woodwork. The faux chinchilla counterpane is a final touch of sheer indulgence.

ream and ice-white taffeta curtains surround the four-poster. The inspiration came from the bed in the Tobacco Room at Nancy Lancaster's Kelmarsh Hall, Northamptonshire, England. It's an updated version of a seventeenth-century state bed with a pelmet so crisp and clean it looks like folded paper. The tassels and ropes are dirty mauve, as is the velvet upholstery on the Swedish stool at the foot of the bed. The headboard is upholstered in a coffee-and-cream-striped taffeta.

This pretty spare room has invitingly crisp white linen sheets and a tailored bed skirt of red-and-white-striped dimity. The curtains at the window, out of view, are in the same striped fabric. The carpet is a Nicholas Haslam design called Dragonfly, which was specially woven in red and white for the room.

Spare bedrooms present a wonderful opportunity to do something pretty and romantic without having to worry about the practicality of huge amounts of storage and wardrobe space. This is the spare room of the mill house shown on pages 68–79. It is in the oldest part of the house, which dates back to the twelfth century. Because it is a small room with low ceilings, I painted it white and limewashed the beams to prevent them from being dark and forbidding. There were plaster shelves in a niche on one side of the bed, so I had a matching set made for the other side to even up the proportions.

The high Queen Anne–style headboard, a stunning example of overscaling, takes up no space at all but has the effect of making the room seem larger. I covered the headboard in the same material that is used for British guardsmen's cloaks, creating a strong, sculptural shape against the white wall.

*An Edwardian fantasy
is rescued from overkill
thanks to the faded colors
of the chintz, the pewter-colored silk-
and-linen carpet, the white woodwork,
and, out of view, a baldaquin bed
curtained in plain pistachio-green silk.*

The principal bedroom of a London town house, pictured here, was almost untouched in its

Edwardian splendor, and I decided to keep that feeling. I used a copy of an Edwardian chintz

everywhere – on the walls, for the curtains, and in the window-seat alcove. The pretty chairs and

the console table have their fair share of glamorous gilding, but it is quite scruffy. The upholstery for

the chairs is the palest pink ribbed silk. I found a very pretty chandelier to hang in the window. It is a

delicate porcelain crown of flowers and ivy leaves with beaded shades – a perfect period piece that

complements the elaborately glazed window. At night, candles flicker in the green-painted iron

appliques (see page 166) on the overmantel.

   The decoration of a bedroom in New Orleans, shown overleaf, was designed around a wonderful

mirror-fronted wardrobe painted with birds and sprays of flowers. The walls and the bed are

covered in a cotton printed with an eighteenth-century design that picks up the foliage beautifully.

I used the cotton on its reverse side for the walls, so it would look washed out and faded, and

the right way around for the bed curtains. I took the cream silk faille curtains right up to the ceiling,

beyond the top of the windows, and echoed the rococo curves of the wardrobe with an

elaborately curved pelmet, edged in prune-colored ribbon to define the shape.

A bedroom inspired by a wardrobe. The cotton shades at the windows are embroidered with a delicate trellis in the room's signature greens and creams with touches of mauve and pink. The French daybed is upholstered in a ribbed cotton and the tapestry pillow is an early Aubusson. In the photograph on the far left, you can just see a strip of the bathroom wallpaper. It's a French eighteenth-century Mauny design in greens and mauves.

Perhaps the ultimate in tablecloths: the silver-gray beaded layer is caught with ermine tails and gilt-bronze medallions, and edged with a fringe that complements both the beadwork and the red-and-gold Jacobean embroidery of the layer beneath.

WIT & WISDOM
the art of detail

The classic solution to the occasional demand for extra seating is the slipper chair, shown near right — a comfortably upholstered, armless chair on casters.

My "Picasso" footstools, pictured far right, look as good together as apart.

SOFAS and seats

Seating should be flexible. A room that is going to spring welcomingly into life has to be able to accommodate everyone. This is where *meubles roulants* come into play – chairs or stools that are comfortable enough to sit on or firm enough to take a tray of drinks, and that you can pull out from a corner or from underneath a table .

In my London apartment I have four footstools that fulfill this purpose. They are very firmly upholstered, and you can actually feel the paint on the surface of the canvas, so it is more like sitting on a painting than on a stool. Together they make up a "Picasso," but they work perfectly well in any combination. They can be put out of the way under a table so I can still enjoy the painting without tripping over them.

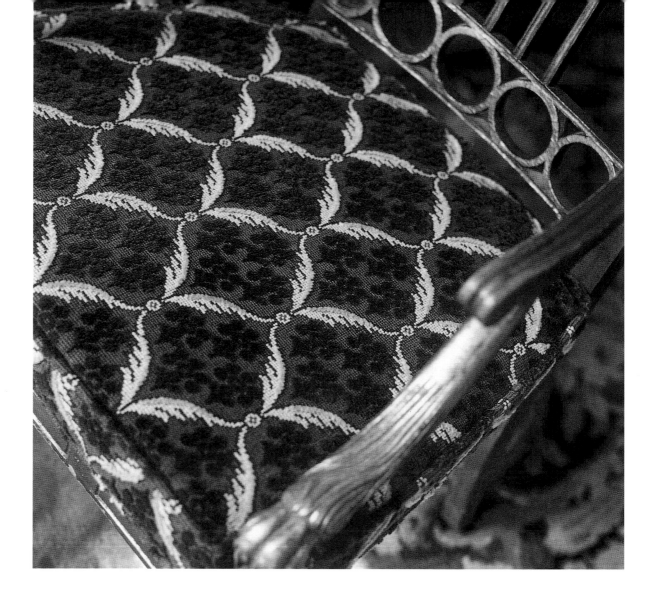

*T*he chair above is upholstered in a
red-and-yellow cut velvet that echoes the
trellis pattern on the chintz sofa, left.
When upholstering with patterns, it is vital to
make sure that the pattern "reads" correctly from
the base of the piece up to the cushions.

Upholstery fabrics that match or "coordinate" are the kiss of death to an original, vibrant room. The trick is to find fabrics that are related in a fairly distant way but complement each other so that the whole is greater than its parts. For this country-house drawing room, I started with a beautiful Savonnerie carpet. Because the room is full of light, I chose a bright yellow-and-pink cotton for the sofa – by day it doesn't look garish and by night it is subtle and rich. Elsewhere in the room, I used red, gold, yellow, and trellis designs.

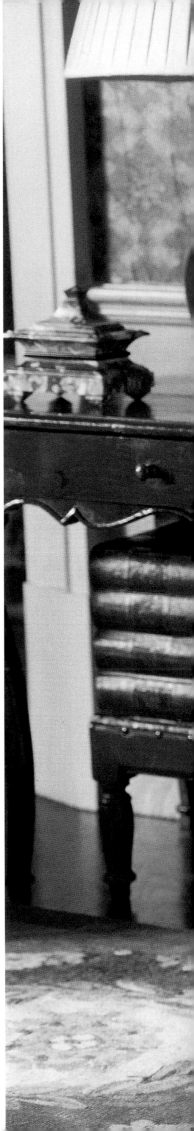

The sofa pictured above is from the drawing room shown on pages 62–63. The big, squashy silk pillows are in different fabrics and differently trimmed. I don't like military rows of identical pillows, which don't look relaxed or inviting, unlike the opulent comfort of the sofa to the right.

I will use tassels, fringes, and ropes on upholstery to define shapes and draw the eye to the proportions of the furniture. I take a great deal of trouble getting the color and the scale of these just right; if they are too small they can look horribly fussy. Good detailing will also help pull a room together – sometimes the dull gleam of a silk rope or the soft edge of an outsized ruffle will make the difference between nice and wonderful.

$\mathscr{P}$ainted furniture is very much part of the Sheer Opulence look. The chair pictured on the left was bought in a sale of Mona Bismarck's furniture on the Isle of Capri. Mona, née Harrison-Williams, was a stylish woman much photographed by Cecil Beaton. The paintwork on this chair is gloriously distressed, and the seat is upholstered in a black, cream, and pink striped silk taffeta.

Another gorgeous eighteenth-century painted chair from the Mona Bismarck sale is shown above left. The fabric was a great find. Almost oriental in the delicacy of its design, it picks up the colors in the chair perfectly.

A slipper chair upholstered in a ribbed shaved velvet, above right, occupies a corner of a small sitting room decorated with chocolate-beige colors. The turquoise piping pulls the elements together smartly.

Dramatic touches in the room above come from the elaborate Chinese chest and
the leopardskin-patterned velvet footstool. The armchair is upholstered in a
prune ottoman silk and the pillow is the color of air. In the white sitting room
on the right, the upholstery is tailored and simple, but the low table most certainly is not.
It is an extravagant mirrored and silvered rococo number from the 1920s.

Marrying up plain fabrics harmoniously takes time and thought. In the white drawing room pictured above, the pattern is largely confined to the floor, as the first purchase I made for this room was a black, yellow, and gold Spanish carpet. Shades of white, mauve, and gray complete the picture. The small sitting room shown at left has a dramatic geometric early Aubusson carpet, 1830s American geometric wallpaper, and upholstery in shades of pale turquoise, prune, gold, and black.

The massive sofa is modern, but its strong lines are timeless and its comfort appealing. The room has whiskey-colored walls and see-through golden-brown metallic curtains lit from behind, so the room looks very dramatic at night. The sofa is upholstered in a toast-colored silk, and the pillows in shades of terra-cotta and orange.

The paneling in this octagonal dining room was inspired by a room in my parents' house. The curtains, which complement the walls, are of taffeta shot with gold and green.

DELICIOUS dining

Dining rooms are essentially nighttime rooms and provide a wonderful opportunity to go all-out for drama. This intimate, theatrical dining room is known as the cabinet. I've made it octagonal with cupboards in the corners and echoed the rhythm of the arched cupboards with the curved pelmet. The rhythm is nicely counterpointed by a pull-up shade of striped see-through silk taffeta.

The centerpiece on the mill house dining table is a tulipière (a tin-glazed earthenware vase) that was found in Barbados. It has white candles in the tulip-shaped candleholders and fresh white tulips arranged in the flower nozzles.

The mill house dining room pictured on pages 72–75 originally had a large fireplace that exaggerated the room's narrow shape. I replaced it with a smaller one, which made the room look pleasingly square, and placed a mirror over it. The mirror leans slightly forward so that it reflects the water outside rather than people standing in front of it. The niches at either side of the fireplace display the collection of beautiful Ludwigsburg porcelain, which continues over the walls.

The painted dining table, a copy of an Arts and Crafts piece, can seat ten when extended. I had found four eighteenth-century dining chairs, and we needed eight. I didn't want the chairs to be all the same because, ranged around the walls, they could make the room look like a municipal boardroom. The four extra chairs therefore are in a different padded design, with button backs. All eight chairs are covered in a pale orange, mauve, and cream geranium-patterned chintz.

DRAPES
and details

Curtains should hang from rods or pelmets to the floor, just breaking on it, never landing in puddles. I like pelmets that drape as if they were carved from wood or plaster. Detailing plays an important part in the overall look – the two examples here show tassels and rope used with artful restraint.

A draped pelmet of heavy silk, left, is topped with a gilded metal fringe and caught with gilded tassels. Above, a bed canopy is outlined with a simple rope-and-tassel arrangement.

Twisted crystal shell-forms are sewn to the bottom edge of a chintz pelmet (left). This pelmet frames a window that looks out directly onto a river, and the crystal catches the play of sunlight on water.

Bedroom curtains in a black floral chintz (right) have been given a fuzzy, funky look with an edging ruffle made from three layers of pink chintz.

Trims, tassels, fringes, and borders need to be used with discretion. When artfully placed, they take the eye instantly to the right place, so the folds of drapery or the sinuous curve of a pelmet can be better appreciated. I like to add touches of the unexpected too – like an outrageous ruffle on a sober curtain or crystal beads dangling from the edge of a pelmet.

A room with a grand cornice sometimes needs a grandly simple pelmet to match. In the dining

room above, which was inspired by chinoiserie panels, the hard pelmet of beige linen has been

shaped and hand-painted to echo the chinoiserie's scrolls. At the other end of the scale from

hand-painted borders, I've often used cheap, gaudy trimmings to great effect – it's all in the styling.

I like to use several layers of curtains: a dress curtain, a pulling curtain, and a voile; then one can

change the mood according to whatever layer seems most appropriate.

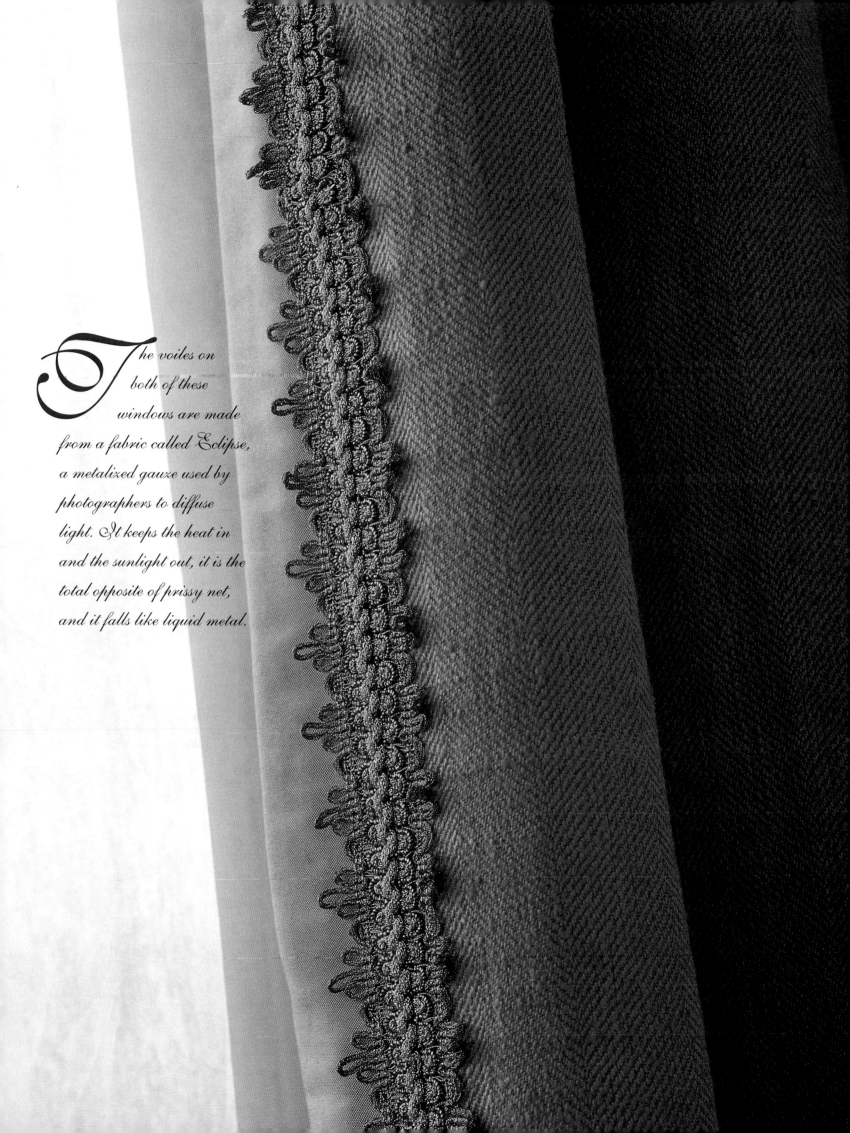

The voiles on both of these windows are made from a fabric called Eclipse, a metalized gauze used by photographers to diffuse light. It keeps the heat in and the sunlight out, it is the total opposite of prissy net, and it falls like liquid metal.

Tassels, fringes, and braids, used with panache, can liven up a plain fabric and tone down a highly patterned one.

MATERIAL heaven

Some designers prefer to start working out a scheme from swatches of material, putting together a sample board of fabrics and finishes for the client's approval. I work in a completely different way, starting with the feel of the room, its proportions, maybe an inspiration from my travels or a key item I want to design the room around. Then I have to find the fabrics to realize the dream. I do have certain fabrics I come back to time and time again, because they work on every level. One of my favorite curtain materials is a cheap linen with a very slight stripe weave that looks like a million dollars and comes in every color imaginable. For furniture I like ribbed silks, cut velvet, and other robust fabrics that will keep their looks; then I'll throw in a little gauzy something as a surprise.

The bolster with the neatly pleated buttoned end (left) is made from a fabric I have just discovered, but you have to scout in Russia for it. It is the cheapest possible cotton mattress ticking in green and mauve stripes.

A tactile bedtime experience is afforded by silk bed curtains, a padded taffeta headboard, and a simple counterpane (right).

The choice of fabric is very important in a bedroom. If I want a fabric to hang in folds that will hold their sculptural looks, I choose a heavy silk or linen. Expensive fabrics do not necessarily work the best. One of my trademark curtain materials is a cheap linen, which, when made up by a genius curtain-maker, looks almost like carved wood. For bed curtains and headboards, I favor the more sensuous velvets, taffetas, and silks. I like headboards to be padded and curvy, and counterpanes to be unfussy. I am not at all keen on cramming a bed with pillows – the prospect of having to remove all of them makes the bed *less* inviting.

The design on this exquisitely beaded and embroidered tablecloth almost floats above the background. Strewn with velvety rose petals, it is a sensational visual experience.

Fabric texture is important too; but texture is not just in the feel and look of something – it is also in the sound. I like active, gritty, grainy textures: wooden tassels that bang against window frames, clattering curtain rings, heavy tassels that fall into place with a satisfying thunk, and metallic fringes that rustle against silk.

The pillow cover on the left was made from the leftover beaded embroidery used for the tablecloth on pages 146–147. It is on a soft brown sofa in a plum-colored sitting room, and its metallic surface picks up every nuance of light.

Three-dimensional velvet paneling has been achieved by covering the wall with cocoa-colored linen velvet, then placing a panel of paler velvet on top and outlining the panel with a thick silk fringe. The chair rail has been left exposed and outlined in braid. It's a very tactile, sensuous wall.

Staircases are about entrances and exits and so deserve to be taken seriously; fabric makes

the most of their potential for drama. Not every house has room for such a splendid focus, but

there are ways to create the illusion of splendor. The staircase on these pages is in a London

mansion apartment, leading from the entrance hall to the mezzanine. I wanted to create the

feeling of opulent splendor that comes from billowing fabric and gleaming metal, so, with a few

yards of fabric and some bronze paint, I created a staircase that cannot be ignored.

A dauntingly dominant staircase needed the Haslam treatment. The wooden handrails were bronzed and the freestanding structure

A section of the "ruin" table shown on pages 102-105 has been pulled apart from the rest and is used here as a serving console. It is a tough-looking item in a clean marble space. A patterned upholstery on the Louis XV chairs would have looked out of place in the outdoor setting, so the chairs have been given linen slipcovers. These are the color of marble, but are textured with random patches as if they had been torn and remade.

TEXTURE

I like really active textures that appeal not only to touch, but to all the senses, and particularly enjoy creating new textural effects by using materials that are not quite what they seem. I like to surprise, for example, with a surface that looks hard, like cold stone or smooth marble, and turns out to be painted wood; or what looks like a carved wooden pelmet but is, in fact, stiff linen.

This opulent console table on the left has a dull gleam to it. Covered in roughly cut, fringed, embossed leather held in place with tough-looking gilt studs, it reminds me of the battle tent of some Magyar prince.

A do-it-yourself textured wallpaper painted silver, right, provides the background for this exquisite hand-painted design.

Using layers and textures is a great way to create light; sometimes you need walls to shimmer, particularly in a dining room that is used mostly at night. Mirrors are the conventional way to achieve this, but they can be a bit relentless – neither soft enough nor sufficiently flattering. I prefer to build up a sheen on the wall covering itself to give an enigmatic, three-dimensional effect that never reads the same from one angle to another.

It pays to be bold with walls. The choice is not just between paint and wallpaper – I often use leather, brown corrugated paper, wax, lead powder, bubble-wrap (not easy), or cut paper strips positioned vertically. I really rather hate murals, unless done in monotone – sepia, for example.

The cushions on these gothic chairs, above, are covered with the *Louis Vuitton* signature fabric more commonly seen on smart luggage. Gilded and painted leather walls, right, have a fascinating shimmer.

*L*uxurious
Louis
Vuitton
fabric has also been used
to cover these dressing
room doors. Leather
handles, brass clasps,
and luggage labels all
add to the illusion of a
stack of personalized
cabin trunks.

Flanking the mirror, white French porcelain vases stand on gilded brackets. These attract the eye upward and draw attention to the wonderful crystal chandelier that hangs over the table.

LIGHT

I like soft, non-directional lighting, especially in dining rooms. Mirrors should reflect the sparkle of candlelight and silver, helping to create a memorable nighttime ambience. But I think it is just as important that they are flattering, as few people actually like to look in mirrors. The paneled mirrors created for this dining room are based on eighteenth-century designs that soften and break up reflections; they are all attached to the wall and divided into rectangular sections, with gilt studs at the joints.

On the main staircase in the old mill house featured on pages 68–79, the light comes from three sources: an oeil de boeuf (bull's-eye) window high in the wall, a chunky iron lantern, and a pair of nineteenth-century French iron appliqués (see page 166) flanking an Elizabethan portrait.

Beautiful lighting is never restricted to formal lamps and chandeliers – indeed, to create the hazy, shimmering atmospheres I love, I turn away from the usual light sources and toward the unconventional, more seductive, reflected light. Lighting social occasions well is vital: I install mirrors in dining rooms which maximize the effects of glittering silverware, opulent spangled crystal, twinkling glassware, and also amplify the glossy chocolate sheen from centuries of polish on antique tables.

*P*ear-tree twigs and an old anchor form the basis of the chandelier that hangs above the Jean Cocteau profile in my own sitting room, above. The tole lantern in the center photo hangs in the entrance hall of a grand London apartment. In this instance the lantern is underscaled to make the entrance hall seem bigger. On the right is one of the four silver lanterns that hang in the corners of the dining room shown on page 43. The rosettes are the color of sealing wax and in the form of double Maltese crosses.

One of a pair of enormous wood-and-metal Italian church chandeliers, right, that hang at either end of the huge drawing room seen on pages 58–61. It is about five feet (1.8 meters) in diameter, but is not overbearing as the construction is so spare. The chain is covered with a brightly colored sleeve that finishes at ceiling level in a Turk's head knot.

On the left, a classic urn is bathed in a pool of light. The gilt-wood girandole on the wall above holds real candles.

I like pretty lights and real candles, which is why I am not really in tune with halogen lamps, floodlights, and spotlights. They have their place, of course, but not in drawing rooms and dining rooms, where people want to look and feel their best. I use a lot of table lamps, as I like the way they create pools of light above and beneath. Overhead lights have to be decorative – either chandeliers or lanterns, and the bigger the better. Wall lights are wonderful because they're like architectural elements you can use to balance proportions, and light that flickers on walls is very flattering. Appliques, which are carved and gilded wall decorations, popular in the eighteenth century, can be turned into wall lights, as can girandoles, which are basically appliques with candlesticks.

$\mathcal{A}$ pair of ridiculously overscaled mirrors completely dominates this small bathroom. The over-the-top frames are richly gilded.

It's common knowledge that mirrors make little rooms appear larger, but large mirrors make even the smallest rooms seem huge. They also make spaces appear brighter because they bounce light around. However, I have always been wary of acres of perfect, pristine mirror glass, especially in bathrooms. Apart from shaving and applying makeup, when a perfect reflection is essential, I think most figures look their best reflected in the kinder light of antiqued glass.

A pair of blue marble bathrooms. The one on the left was inspired by the ballroom in the Neues Palais at Potsdam, and I used similar colors in the room above to maximize space.

A beautiful gilt-bronze dolphin chandelier hangs above this marble and faux marble bath like a waterfall. The azure blue walls are marbleized with veins of gold and highlighted with gilt-bronze details – appliques (see page 166) and door hardware. White taffeta curtains are made to look as if they are permanently blowing in the wind.

INDEX

Page numbers refer to text and captions.
Abbreviations: NH (Nicholas Haslam)

AUTHOR'S ACKNOWLEDGMENTS

For the creation of this book, I first have to express my profound gratitude to all the clients, past and present, who have so generously allowed their homes to be photographed, and for being a constant source of inspiration, friendship and delight.

This book would not have come to fruition without the constant badgering of my friend David Montgomery, who had the initial idea of a defining volume of my work, and then spent several late nights and early mornings devising many of the beautiful photographs contained in these pages.

I also sincerely wish to thank my wonderful design team, and many craftsmen, artists and suppliers around the world, who have been so readily understanding and peerlessly efficient in helping me achieve these unique interiors.

PUBLISHERS' ACKNOWLEDGMENTS

The publishers would particularly like to thank Flora Connell, Nicholas Haslam's incomparable Personal Assistant, for her charm, efficiency, kindness and expertise throughout the whole of the making of this book.

Special thanks go to Cynthia Inions for matchless styling, to David Montgomery for his exquisite photography, to Peter Chan for his dedication and enthusiasm as David's assistant, and to Karen Howes for her invaluable help with picture research. The publishers would also like to thank Go Airways.

PHOTOGRAPHIC ACKNOWLEDGMENTS

All photographs are in the book are by David Montgomery and are © Cico Books,
    except for those that appear on the following pages:
Pages 9, 10 © The Country Life Picture Library
Pages 24-5, 26-7 © Simon Upton –The Interior Archive
Pages 80-81, 82, 83, 84-85 116, 117 © Andrew Wood –The Interior Archive
Pages 28, 29, 30–31, 32-33, 94-95, 96–97, 98-99, 100-101, 106- 107
    © Fritz von der Schulenburg –The Interior Archive
Pages 34-35, 36–37, © Christopher Simon Sykes – The Interior Archive

The watercolor paintings that appear on pages 7–17 are © Nicholas Haslam